Arctic Hares

Therese Shea

Gareth Stevens
Publishing

Please visit our Web site, www.garethstevens.com. For a free color catalog of all our high-quality books, call toll free 1-800-542-2595 or fax 1-877-542-2596.

Library of Congress Cataloging-in-Publication Data

Shea, Therese.
 Arctic hares / Therese Shea.
   p. cm. – (Animals that live in the tundra)
 Includes index.
 ISBN 978-1-4339-3891-7 (pbk.)
 ISBN 978-1-4339-3892-4 (6-pack)
 ISBN 978-1-4339-3890-0 (library binding)
 1. Arctic hare–Juvenile literature. I. Title.
 QL737.L32S46 2011
 599.32'8–dc22

                                            2010013802

First Edition

Published in 2011 by
Gareth Stevens Publishing
111 East 14th Street, Suite 349
New York, NY 10003

Designer: Michael J. Flynn
Editor: Therese Shea

Photo credits: Cover, pp. 1, 13 (both), 21, back cover Shutterstock.com; p. 5 Wayne R. Bilenduke/The Image Bank/Getty Images; p. 7 Paul J. Richards/ AFP/Getty Images; p. 9 Norbert Rosing/National Geographic/Getty Images; pp. 11, 15 Nick Norman/National Geographic/Getty Images; p. 17 Jerry Kobalenko/ Photographer's Choice/Getty Images; p. 19 Art Wolfe/Stone/Getty Images.

Printed in the United States of America

CPSIA compliance information: Batch #CS10GS: For further information contact Gareth Stevens, New York, New York at 1-800-542-2595.

Table of Contents

Boldface words appear in the glossary.

Where's the Hare?

What is cute, furry, and hops around one of the coldest places on Earth? An arctic hare! Arctic hares live in the Arctic **tundra**.

Arctic hares have thick fur that keeps them warm in the cold tundra. Their fur is white in winter to blend in with snow and ice.

In summer, arctic hares **shed** their white fur. Under the white fur is gray or brown fur. It blends in with the land after the snow melts.

shedding hare

Long Legs

Hares have longer back legs than rabbits do. Arctic hares stand on their back legs to look for danger.

long back legs

Arctic hares can run very fast. Their speed helps them escape arctic foxes and arctic wolves. Sometimes they hold their front legs up and hop like kangaroos!

arctic wolf

arctic fox

When they rest, arctic hares sit on their legs. They flatten their ears, too. This helps keep in their body heat.

Finding Food

Arctic hares eat plants, roots, mosses, bark, and berries. In winter, they use their sharp nails to dig through the snow and ice to find food.

Bucks and Does

Arctic hares find **mates** in spring. **Male** hares are called bucks. Bucks may fight for mates. They stand on their back legs and "box"!

Female arctic hares are called does (DOHZ). They build nests of fur and grass. They have babies in spring or summer. The babies are full grown by fall.

Fast Facts

Length	up to 26 inches (66 centimeters) from head to rear; tail, up to 3 inches (8 centimeters)
Weight	up to 15 pounds (7 kilograms)
Speed	up to 40 miles (65 kilometers) per hour
Diet	plants, mosses, bark, berries, and roots
Average life span	about 5 years

Glossary

female: a girl

male: a boy

mate: one of a pair of animals that come together to make a baby

shed: to lose hair

tundra: flat, treeless plain with ground that is always frozen

For More Information

Books

Frost, Helen. *Arctic Hares.* Mankato, MN: Capstone Press, 2007.

Spinelli, Eileen. *Polar Bear, Arctic Hare: Poems of the Frozen North.* Honesdale, PA: Wordsong, 2007.

Web Sites

Arctic Hare
animals.nationalgeographic.com/animals/mammals/arctic-hare
Find out why arctic hares have long been important to Native Americans.

Cool Critters
www.alaskakids.org/index.cfm?section=Cool-Critters&page=Featured-Critters
Read about arctic hares and other animals that live in Alaska.

Publisher's note to educators and parents: Our editors have carefully reviewed these Web sites to ensure that they are suitable for students. Many Web sites change frequently, however, and we cannot guarantee that a site's future contents will continue to meet our high standards of quality and educational value. Be advised that students should be closely supervised whenever they access the Internet.

Index

About the Author

Therese Shea is an editor and author of many children's nonfiction books. A graduate of Providence College, she has an M.A. in English Education from the University at Buffalo. She lives and works in Buffalo, New York.